W9-BLO-468

Drug Abuse and Society™

OXYCONTIN™

From Pain Relief to Addiction

The Rosen Publishing Group, Inc., New York

Brad Lockwood

To you, youth, our future

Published in 2007 by The Rosen Publishing Group, Inc.
29 East 21st Street, New York, NY 10010

Library of Congress Cataloging-in-Publication Data

Lockwood, Brad.
OxyContin: from pain relief to addiction / Brad Lockwood.—1st ed.
    p. cm.—(Drug abuse and society)
Includes bibliographical references and index.
ISBN-13: 978-1-4042-0913-8
ISBN-10: 1-4042-0913-1 (lib. bdg.)
1. Oxycodone. 2. Oxycodone abuse.
I. Title. II. Series.
RM666.O76L63 2006
615'.32335—dc22

                                        2006008394

Manufactured in the United States of America

Contents

INTRODUCTION

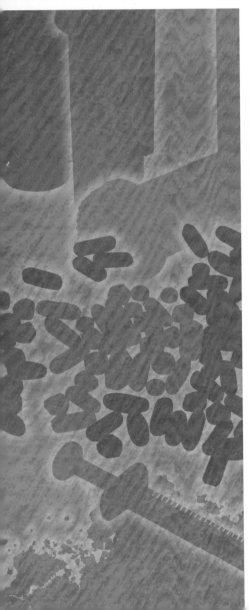

Relief from chronic pain has long been a major problem for both patients and doctors. Pain is difficult to treat accurately. Plus, pain is relative to the individual. There is no measure or scale of a person's discomfort, which forces doctors to trust their patients while trying to treat them. In industries like coal mining, lumber, fishing, and construction, workers are more likely to suffer from long-term injuries, broken bones, damaged joints, and aching backs. This leaves laborers disabled by severe pain, and doctors looking for a cure.

Those in even more need of pain relief are cancer patients, who often suffer excruciating pain from the disease as well from the lengthy treatments needed to cure it. For decades the major sources of

The steel worker in this photograph cuts through a billet (a long, unfinished length of steel) glowing at 2,000 degrees Fahrenheit (1,093 degrees Celsius) at the TAMCO steel mill in Rancho Cucamonga, California. Industrial workers, often the victims of job-related injuries, were the first large group of OxyContin users.

relief have been prescriptions of powerful opium-based drugs (opiates) that are also highly addictive. Balancing a patient's need for pain relief with his or her potential for addiction has been a recurring problem with all opiates.

Thanks to modern breakthroughs in synthetic drugs, however, this balancing act seemed to be heading toward a solution. In the 1990s, oxycodone, a synthetic opiate (known as an opioid) was developed. Derived from opiates, opioids like oxycodone promised the perfect solution: long-term relief from chronic pain with few instances of addiction. Without concern for addiction, doctors started prescribing oxycodone-based drugs almost immediately.

Oxycodone-based drugs include Percocet, Percodan, Tylox, and OxyContin. Introduced in 1995 by the pharmaceutical company Purdue Pharma, OxyContin tablets contain substantially larger doses of oxycodone. Percocet, Percodan, and Tylox contain 5 milligrams of oxycodone versus from 10 to 160 milligrams in OxyContin. Obviously intended for severe pain, OxyContin became the preferred medication for chronic pain sufferers and cancer patients because it was so powerful. Doctors appreciated that OxyContin, when taken as prescribed, offered little chance of addiction. As a result, Purdue Pharma heavily marketed its new "miracle" drug. Doctors enthusiastically prescribed OxyContin—not only to treat cancer patients but to help others who were healing from minor injuries, like those occurring in a fall, or a chronic backache.

Incredibly powerful for patients and highly profitable for Purdue Pharma, OxyContin was, indeed, a miracle drug, until people began abusing it. Taken as a tablet as prescribed, the oxycodone in OxyContin is released gradually over a twelve-hour period. This extended release makes OxyContin's high dosage acceptable, offering effective, long-lasting pain relief. But when altered in any way, the drug did the opposite. When altered, OxyContin produces an immediate high, which makes people feel relaxed and numb. These feelings are similar to the effects of heroin, a highly addictive opiate. When used in ways not intended by the pharmaceutical company, OxyContin is actually highly addictive. Instances of abuse of OxyContin as an illegal, misused drug became as plentiful as its legal use by patients for treating pain.

This situation was most unusual—having a drug being prescribed for its safe and effective properties, but also leading to abuse if altered. Mass-marketed by Purdue Pharma to doctors across the country, the drug eventually found its way into the medicine cabinets of tens of thousands of homes. Altering OxyContin to increase its effects quickly became an epidemic that continues today.

The problems started in small, blue-collar towns where labor-intensive industries lead to accidents and injuries. OxyContin's popularity in these regions soon gave it the nickname "hillbilly heroin." And because its manufacturer has made large sums of money from OxyContin and continues to market it heavily—as well as fight lawsuits and attempts to pull it off the market—Purdue Pharma, in some people's opinion, has earned a somewhat dubious reputation.

Today, treatment centers across the United States report abnormal increases in OxyContin addiction. In many states, methadone clinics are treating more OxyContin patients than heroin addicts. Known on the street as "Oxy," "O.C.," or even "killer,"

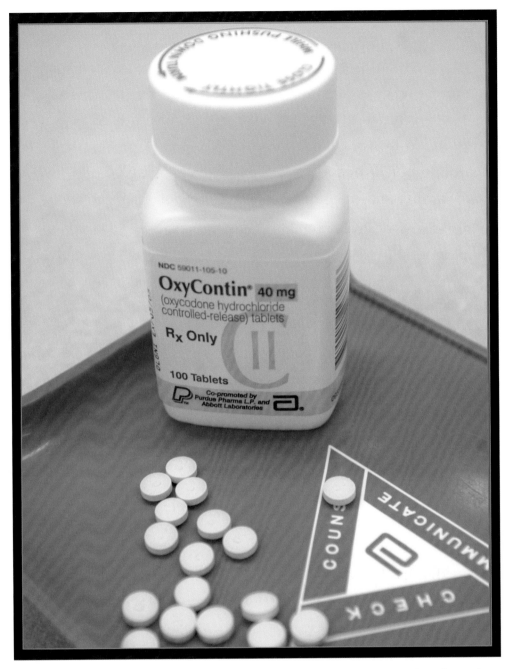

OxyContin, seen in this 2001 photograph, has an extremely high value when sold illegally on the street. The powerful painkiller, which is being used by some addicts to achieve a high similar to a heroin rush, became extremely popular within a few years of its invention.

OxyContin has led to many deaths. In Massachusetts alone, from 1999 to 2003, opioid-related deaths jumped from 94 to 574, according to the Massachusetts Department of Public Health. This is a dramatic increase for synthetic opioids versus opiates. Mostly due to mixing OxyContin with alcohol or other drugs, the total number of fatalities attributed to the drug is nearly impossible to calculate because data about abuse from opiates and opioids are combined for tracking by law enforcement. But conservative estimates exceed 10,000 for both opioids and opiates since the 1990s, when opioids were first introduced.

Comprehensive news reports such as a 2005 story about OxyContin on National Public Radio's *All Things Considered* claim that "one in twenty high school seniors acknowledges taking OxyContin." The story cited data from the 2005 Monitoring the Future Study by the National Institute on Drug Abuse (NIDA). According to that report, "OxyContin use by [high-school] seniors has increased by 40 percent over the past three years." This new data claims that there are five times more OxyContin users than methamphetamine users, the widely abused and potent street stimulant that has been popularized by young people in recent years.

In one Boston suburb, high school journalists took a poll in 2006 to estimate the extent of drug abuse among fellow students for an article in their school newspaper. What they found alarmed them: OxyContin was by far the greatest source of the students' drug problems. Some 17 percent of teens claimed to have experimented with the drug. More and more polls have found that people of all ages believe that OxyContin is a "safer" high than street drugs because it has been professionally manufactured. The trouble is that abusers are not taking the drug as prescribed. And some abusers have not been prescribed the drug at all. Plus, many people alter the pills to heighten their effects, breaking down their ability to be released throughout the body over long periods.

The rapidly expanding OxyContin epidemic may be one of the worst in many years. Although Purdue Pharma has introduced new versions of OxyContin to limit abuse of the drug, these are only now becoming available. Meanwhile, patients suffering from chronic pain still praise OxyContin—which remains safe, effective, and non-addictive when used properly—just as doctors continue to prescribe it for the same reasons. Still, many doctors have been arrested and convicted for writing prescriptions for addicts. A single OxyContin tablet, legally purchased at the pharmacy for about fifty cents, can be illegally sold for up to $80—profits that feed illegal sales by drug dealers. Pharmacies, homes, and patients have all been robbed to support the OxyContin epidemic.

OxyContin abuse is forcing many people to ask serious questions. Does mass abuse by addicts outweigh the benefits of chronic pain relief for patients? Should a pharmaceutical company be held liable for creating a product that can be highly addictive if it's misused?

CHAPTER 1

Societal Trends

For all of the breakthroughs in medicine, including drugs, technology, treatment, and training, the actual pain being experienced by a patient cannot be accurately measured. The extent of a person's suffering can only be expressed verbally. One person's pain may be another person's mild discomfort, or vice versa. Pain is relative to each sufferer, leaving doctors somewhat ill equipped to assess its level.

Certain injuries, illnesses, and treatments are inherently linked to pain. Cancer patients often suffer incredible discomfort while undergoing treatment, while serious accidents in specific high-risk jobs can result in the same. Back injuries, muscle tears, joint damage, and broken bones frequently occur in blue-collar occupations like mining, lumbering, fishing, and construction. Other jobs like shipping (continually lifting heavy packages) have also left workers with long-term pain. Cancer does not discriminate, but in certain rural regions with labor-intensive industries, chronic pain has left large populations suffering to the point of being disabled.

Aspirin, acetaminophen, and ibuprofen alone do not alleviate chronic pain. Plus, constantly taking over-the-counter pain

Because OxyContin rose in popularity quickly, its use and misuse also increased tremendously, spurring a string of pharmacy robberies nationwide. Many pharmacists now take measures to lock up OxyContin in an effort to discourage theft of the drug and reduce insurance costs.

relievers regularly leads to other problems including damage to the stomach lining, kidneys, and liver. For decades, the only way to address chronic pain was by prescribing powerful opium-based drugs like codeine and, in the most severe cases, morphine. However effective, opiates regularly led to abuse because they are also highly addictive. Perhaps the most problematic example of opiate addiction is heroin, an illicit drug that has been hooking abusers for nearly a century. Unlike many codeine and morphine abusers, however, pain sufferers do not regularly become heroin abusers.

THE "MIRACLE" DRUG

For decades, the addictive side effects of opiates have been accepted because these drugs made patients more comfortable after an injury, surgery, or serious illness. A "cure-all" drug—a medication that alleviated pain without addiction—was but a dream. In the early 1990s, however, this dream suddenly became possible. Synthetic opiates, known as opioids, were the latest, and seemingly greatest, of the new medical discoveries. Like opiates, opioids alleviated chronic pain for longer periods, but amazingly, early tests showed little, if any, chance of addiction. By depressing the central nervous system in the body through time-released doses of the opioid oxycodone, pain relief was suddenly available without patients facing the risk of becoming addicted.

Oxycodone, the active opioid ingredient in these new drugs, promised remarkable potential. An early 1990s study of oxycodone by the NIDA of 12,000 patients showed that only four became addicted. Apparently proving the effectiveness of opioids—treating pain relief without addiction—oxycodone-based drugs such as Tylox, Percocet, Percodan, and later, OxyContin, hit the market. The promise of such drugs was further bolstered by the belief among medical professionals that patients experiencing chronic pain would be less likely to become hooked on opioids because their pain was so intense. Ultimately, the opioid oxycodone received unanimous approval. Time-released over a twelve-hour period, one OxyContin tablet promised long-term relief from pain, without the manufacturer, doctor, or patient having to worry about possible addiction.

Purdue Pharma, a Connecticut-based pharmaceutical manufacturer, first introduced OxyContin in 1995. While Tylox and Percocet contain only 5 milligrams of oxycodone, OxyContin contains between 10 and 160 milligrams. Because the large doses of oxycodone are released over time, doctors had little fear of administering such a potent drug. More so, such controlled yet significant pain relief from two pills each day incited more widespread use by patients. Instead of only prescribing oxycodone for cancer patients, doctors began writing prescriptions for OxyContin to treat many conditions for which chronic pain was a symptom. Purdue Pharma encouraged this widespread use by mailing 14,000 videos titled

Cancer patients, like the woman shown here with her doctor, are frequently prescribed drugs such as OxyContin to help them manage the pain associated with both the disease and its treatment. The timed-release component of OxyContin's chemical design allows people who suffer from chronic diseases to be free of pain for long periods.

I Got My Life Back to doctors and pharmaceutical reps and hosting seminars for doctors to promote sales of its "miracle" drug.

OxyContin prescriptions flooded the market over the next few years, with rural, blue-collar states like Maine, West Virginia, Arkansas, and Washington becoming the primary recipients. Purdue Pharma continued to market its highly powerful and profitable new drug, expanding prescriptions into other states. By

2000, according to a 2002 article in *National Journal*, OxyContin ranked thirty-six among all prescribed drugs that number in the thousands and treat any number of problems including allergies, infections, and insomnia, but not pain. In that area, OxyContin was the number one choice. With more than 7 million total prescriptions, OxyContin became the most popular brand-name narcotic medication for treating moderate-to-severe pain in the United States. In 2001, sales of OxyContin by Purdue Pharma totaled nearly $1.5 billion. By 2005, 1.5 million prescriptions for oxycodone-based drugs were written in Massachusetts alone: that's one prescription for every four residents.

TOO MANY PRESCRIPTIONS

To fully understand the rapid growth of OxyContin use, one must first understand what is considered normal prescription drug use. In 2000, the U.S. Drug Enforcement Administration (DEA) reported that the national average of OxyContin use was 3,704 grams per 100,000 residents. However, in the coalfield counties of southwest Virginia, that average was nearly eight times greater: 25,000 grams per 100,000 residents. The fact that residents in these regions did hard, labor-intensive work that led to more injuries was one reason for such a dramatic increase in OxyContin prescriptions, but something else was obviously amiss.

Early indications of opioid addiction were either unknown or were being downplayed. Along with the earlier NIDA study showing only 4 of 12,000 oxycodone users becoming addicted, another NIDA study published in 2001 under the vague title "Pain Medications: 13553" was overlooked. Of 38 chronic pain patients receiving general opioids for four to seven years, 2 became addicted. Apparently confirming the potential risk of opioid addiction to a greater number of users, this study also highlighted one important factor: both of the patients who became addicted had prior histories of drug abuse. Underreported, this study revealed a serious problem with opioids—that people susceptible to abusing drugs are more prone to becoming addicted to opioids—especially to the high doses available in OxyContin.

Had doctors known that approximately 5 percent of patients had drug abuse problems in the past and should not be given opioids, they may have not prescribed them so often, or at least done more thorough screening of their patients' histories. In reality, OxyContin should have only been prescribed to patients with severe pain who had no prior history of drug abuse. Still, some former addicts who needed the long-term benefits of OxyContin suddenly began falling victim to this susceptibility.

MISUSE OF OXYCONTIN

Another problem with OxyContin soon emerged. When taken as instructed, in whole tablet form, twice each day and only when needed, OxyContin works wonders for those in excruciating pain. But when altered by abusers, OxyContin offers a high akin to its opiate relative, heroin. Even cutting a tablet in half undermines the time-release formula, heightening the dose with unpredictable results.

An immediate floating feeling and numbness with possible hallucinations result from misuse of OxyContin. Unlike heroin, however, OxyContin is prescribed by doctors and covered by insurance companies. The drug soon found its way into medicine

Former DEA executive Asa Hutchinson holds a pen with a pull-out advertisement for OxyContin while testifying on Capitol Hill on December 11, 2001. Hutchinson continued his testimony by insisting that OxyContin abuse was a growing problem in America, resulting in at least 117 known overdose deaths in 2001 alone.

cabinets throughout the United States. Since prescription OxyContin is inexpensive and readily available, some teenagers and young adults began stealing tablets from their parents, relatives, friends, and neighbors to take themselves or sell to others. The sudden mass availability of OxyContin contributed to an increase in the drug's use and misuse creating countless overdoses, some resulting in death.

If you take too many, or alter them in any way, OxyContin pills can be lethal. A cancer patient who has been taking the drug for a while, for example, can take much more OxyContin than a non-user can because of his or her higher tolerance for the drug. Tolerance means that patients who take OxyContin for extended periods will eventually require more and more of the drug to sustain the same amount of pain relief. By contrast, a person taking OxyContin for the first time has little to no tolerance for it. If a non-user ingests the same amount as a cancer patient, he or she could overdose.

The profitability in illegally dealing and selling OxyContin only fed the growing problem. A 100-tablet bottle can be legally purchased with a prescription at a pharmacy for around $400. Usually covered by insurance, OxyContin often costs a pain sufferer very little for several weeks of relief. However, the same 100-tablet bottle can also be resold illegally to drug dealers for $2,000–$4,000. OxyContin's high street value was fueling the misuse and illegal selling of the drug. Still, actual law enforcement data is unavailable since official figures combine information related to both opioids and opiates. Beyond teenagers and others stealing pills from patients, the black market for OxyContin was likely supplied early on by both errant patients and doctors seeking quick cash.

MYTHS AND FACTS ABOUT OXYCONTIN

Myth: Opioids like OxyContin have been proven to be less addictive than opiates like heroin.

Fact: When taken as a whole tablet or pill, the opioid oxycodone in OxyContin is time-released to treat long-term, chronic pain. But when OxyContin tablets are altered, the opioids in OxyContin are highly addictive, just like heroin.

Myth: My dad takes OxyContin for pain, so it's okay for me to take it for pain, too.

Fact: OxyContin is the most powerful opioid, and it is only available legally by prescription. Only cancer patients and those suffering severe injuries or chronic pain should take OxyContin, which should be administered by and under a doctor's care.

Myth: Prescription drugs are safe or they wouldn't be legally available.

Fact: Prescription drugs must be prescribed by a doctor because they are powerful and intended to treat specific health problems. It's even more dangerous to mix prescription drugs with other drugs and/or alcohol.

Mixing medication with other drugs or alcohol can have unpredictable, and sometimes fatal, results. In fact, the vast majority of OxyContin-related deaths are due to mixing it with other drugs and/or alcohol.

As is true in many other epidemics, the number of people becoming addicted to OxyContin in low-populated areas was dangerously underreported. Because OxyContin prescriptions were so popular in factory towns, word of the growing instance of addiction and overdose did not spread as quickly as it may have in cities or suburbs. Initially considered a "blue-collar" problem, OxyContin abuse soon spread.

Within a few years, dealers and addicts were all too eager to get OxyContin. The *Journal of Analytical Toxicology* reported that there were 919 OxyContin-related deaths in the United States between 2000 and 2003. These numbers would quickly double, then triple—a ratio that was proportional to the increase in legitimate prescriptions.

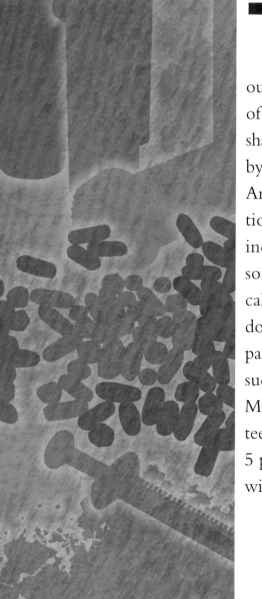

CHAPTER 2

Users and Pushers

The United States, its medical community, pharmaceutical companies, and patients were now in a precarious position. Over the last decade, the abuse of prescription drugs in America has risen sharply. According to a 2004 study released by the Partnership for a Drug-Free America, more students now use prescription drugs than any other substances, including crack, cocaine, and heroin. In some circles, today's teens are now being called "Generation Rx." This epidemic does not only involve OxyContin, but painkillers such as Vicodin and sedatives such as Ambien. For example, a 2005 Monitoring the Future survey about teenage drug use indicated that more than 5 percent of teenagers had used OxyContin without a prescription during the last year.

According to figures recorded by the U.S. Department of Health and Human Services in 2002, approximately 1.9 million people age twelve or older used OxyContin for recreational purposes at least once. In many cases, teenagers are stealing the drugs directly from parents, grandparents, and other relatives.

In the same study, more than 7 percent of teens claimed to be casual users of prescription sedatives. More and more, prescription drugs are being promoted as the cure to any ailment. They are vigorously advertised on television, over the Internet, and even touted by some doctors who are sometimes encouraged by representatives from pharmaceutical companies.

A 2003 report issued by the Government Accountability Office (GAO) titled "Prescription Drugs: OxyContin Abuse and

Diversion and Efforts to Address the Problem" showed that "more than 31 million Americans admitted having used prescription drugs for non-medical reasons . . ." This study also cited a dramatic increase in this illicit behavior over the prior year: 1.6 million more Americans reported misusing and/or abusing prescription drugs. Specific to OxyContin, non-medical abuse increased in this same period from 11.8 million in 2002 to 13.7 million in 2003. Underscoring the seriousness of this epidemic, a study by the U.S. Department of Health and Human Services showed a large jump in deaths in hospital emergency rooms due to prescription drugs in more than half of the cities in the United States. Overall, the study found misuse of painkillers accounted for 10 percent of all emergency room visits in 2002, an increase of more than 160 percent from 1995.

As powerful as they are plentiful, prescription drugs have increased in use and abuse. Addiction increases insurance premiums and is at least partially responsible for the rising costs of health care. Plus, drug abuse reaches the highest levels of business, entertainment, and government. Radio talk-show host Rush Limbaugh admitted an addiction to painkillers, and settled felony charges in April 2006, paying fines and accepting an eighteen-month probationary rehabilitation program. Even Vice President Dick Cheney dismissed his personal physician for abusing prescription drugs. In a separate incident, President George W. Bush's niece Noelle Bush, who is Florida governor Jeb Bush's daughter, was arrested for trying to use a fake prescription to

Radio personality Rush Limbaugh in 2003 admitted to being addicted to painkillers, especially OxyContin. He made the news again in 2006, when he was arrested for allegedly "doctor shopping" for prescriptions. As part of his plea-bargain agreement, the commentator must continue drug rehabilitation for eighteen months and pay a fine of $30,000.

buy the anti-anxiety drug Xanax. However public or private, the impact of prescription drug abuse on all Americans is overwhelming.

Yet OxyContin abuse also impacts the most needy and least likely: injured hard-working laborers and cancer patients facing excruciating pain, as well as the doctors trying to treat them. Due to the misuse and abuse of OxyContin by black-market selling and dealing, the drug is now shrouded in suspicion. Dozens of doctors have been arrested and jailed for writing prescriptions to known addicts. Purdue Pharma continues to face civil lawsuits and millions of dollars in potential fines and settlements, each one involving OxyContin abuse. Ironically, the OxyContin epidemic brought about one positive aspect—a new awareness to the dangers of prescription drugs.

OXYCONTIN AND HEROIN

The initial market for OxyContin (cancer patients and chronic pain sufferers) is no longer the only market for the drug. Successful professionals from wealthy suburbs were suddenly abusing OxyContin. The fact that OxyContin is readily available in many households is one reason for the increase in its use, but its street value is another.

Sold legally at pharmacies for approximately $400 for 100 tablets, OxyContin is not inexpensive. On the black market, with each tablet legally costing under 50¢ (or less after insurance match payments), the drug can be resold illegally for up to $80 a tablet. OxyContin can lead to an addiction that is as costly as it is dangerous. OxyContin abuse quickly expanded from rural regions into suburbs and cities. Soon, people from all races and professions were "doctor shopping" to get OxyContin. ("Doctor shopping" is going from one doctor to another and describing the same symptoms in order to obtain enough prescriptions to ensure a regular supply of the drug.)

Ultimately, when no other doctors will comply with a patient's demand for more pills, his or her drive to supply an addiction can lead to the abuse of street drugs with similar effects, such as heroin. The typical OxyContin abuser has an average income above $20,000, which is much higher than that of the average heroin user. However, the two share much in common.

Perhaps the most serious result of OxyContin abuse is the tendency of users to turn to alternative, less expensive drugs to get high. And because OxyContin is expensive, and heroin is relatively cheap, some users start with OxyContin and then turn to heroin. Among Americans age twelve and older studied in 2002 and 2003, 1.7 million had used both heroin and OxyContin, according to the National Household Survey on Drug Abuse (NHSDA).

OxyContin and heroin abusers are predominantly white and age thirty-five and older. Many people who start using OxyContin after an injury or illness claim to report never having considered using heroin. However, they either run out of money or become unable to get prescriptions. Thus, some invariably turn to heroin. They usually have good jobs and no arrest records. This has baffled law enforcement authorities because OxyContin abusers are the least likely addicts and criminals— that is until they can't get any more pills.

Both OxyContin and heroin abusers suffer withdrawal from addiction. To stop abusing such drugs, professional treatment is necessary to help curb withdrawal symptoms. Treatment for both OxyContin and heroin abuse can take months. It also requires supervision since addicts are often given other drugs (mostly methadone, a synthetic narcotic that has fewer side effects during withdrawal) to ease the body's withdrawal symptoms. Addicts in withdrawal experience cold and hot flashes, uncontrolled sweating, headaches akin to migraines, and constant vomiting. This is why most OxyContin addicts go to methadone clinics to recover, just as heroin addicts do.

Recent studies continue to show that OxyContin abuse is significant among young people—most likely leading to increased heroin abuse in the future. Use of other, illegal drugs has decreased among teenagers (alcohol, steroids, even methamphetamine), while, according to the 2005 Monitoring the Future study, OxyContin use by twelfth graders increased by 40 percent. Of further concern is the reality that these teenage addicts know at least one person who has overdosed and/or died from OxyContin or heroin. Despite these grave warnings, abuse of prescription drugs continues to grow, leading authorities to take a hard look at who is pushing these powerful, often dangerous—even fatal—medications.

PROFESSIONAL PUSHER

OxyContin is a powerful drug with a high "street" value, making illegal sales profitable and problematic. Consistent supplies of OxyContin for dealing are difficult to obtain because prescriptions are required. Pharmacies and doctors are usually on the lookout for potential OxyContin abusers, so who is supplying the street trade? Surprisingly, law enforcement authorities have found that some doctors are doing the "pushing."

From 2001 to 2002, the DEA initiated 257 OxyContin-related abuse and diversion cases resulting in 302 arrests and more than $1 million in fines. (A case termed "diversion" means that drugs originally intended to treat one problem are being used or resold for an alternative use.) Medicare officials in states across the country have undertaken similar enforcement efforts, resulting in many arrests and convictions. Although these numbers pale in comparison to arrests for selling marijuana and cocaine, many of those being caught are actually doctors. In fact, the doctor who wrote the most prescriptions for OxyContin that were covered by Medicare was arrested, had his license suspended, and now faces jail time. He was not only arrested for abusing his ability to write prescriptions, but for manslaughter, because some of his patients overdosed and died.

"Dr. Feelgood"

Rumors spread that patients of Dr. James Graves held tailgate parties in his office parking lot in Florida, awaiting their appointments. Wanting a steady fix, Graves's patients were his biggest fans, but for the wrong reasons. In Florida, if you wanted OxyContin, you went to Dr. Graves.

The total number of prescriptions that Dr. Graves wrote for OxyContin is unknown; however four deaths resulted from those prescriptions. Two of the four people died within hours of obtaining the pills. Both ended up dead as the result of overdoses, as did the other two later. As for Dr. Graves, he faces the rest of his life in prison.

"He is no different than a drug dealer," said the prosecutor during Graves's trial. Though Dr. Graves tried to defend himself, saying he was a reputable professional who was misled by these drug-abusing patients, he was found guilty on all counts. This included one count for racketeering, five for unlawful delivery of a controlled substance, and, most serious of all, four counts of manslaughter. Dr. Graves was convicted and sentenced to sixty-three years in prison.

This is not an isolated case, however. Dozens of doctors face stiff fines and time behind bars for prescribing narcotics to known abusers. However, many doctors say it is unfair to prosecute them for prescribing drugs to patients who may be lying about their symptoms or going from doctor to doctor for multiple prescriptions.

Cases of doctors being arrested for writing OxyContin prescriptions are widespread. The DEA approaches this particular problem differently from most others by targeting the doctors who write prescriptions for known drug abusers. Meanwhile, medical professionals are defending the rights of patients who need the drug for legitimate pain relief. Some patients in true need are having trouble getting prescriptions because of all the scrutiny surrounding OxyContin. This debate is ongoing, as is the spread of OxyContin addiction.

Given such debate, the manufacturer of OxyContin, Purdue Pharma, also faces scrutiny. A December 2003 report to Congress by the U.S. GAO cited the company for its "overly aggressive marketing" of OxyContin.

In an unusual development, federal courts have started making pharmaceutical companies liable for the misuse of the drugs they manufacture, most notably Merck for the anti-inflammatory drug Vioxx. Purdue Pharma did heavily market OxyContin. Seventy percent of the company's revenues came from sales of this one painkiller. In its advertising campaign, it mailed videos, offered seminars, hired hundreds of salespeople, and advertised OxyContin to doctors as a "miracle drug."

By claiming that people other than cancer patients and serious pain sufferers could benefit from OxyContin, most doctors, lawyers, and juries seem to agree that Purdue Pharma bears at least some responsibility for the current abuse. The company has settled some of these claims, but it still faces additional civil lawsuits for its actions. However, Purdue Pharma never directly marketed OxyContin to the public, only to doctors, making them equally liable.

CHAPTER 3
Human Behavior and Addiction

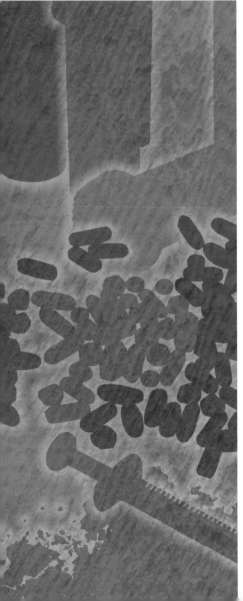

Sam was a seventeen-year-old athlete. Megan was a fifty-year-old homemaker. Even with their difference in age, these two people shared a distinct habit: they both got hooked on painkillers, and eventually, OxyContin.

Sam had been injured in a football game, leaving him with lightning bolts of pain shooting through his back. Around the same time, Megan slipped on the stairs and injured her hip, leaving her in constant discomfort. Both Sam and Megan went to their doctors for help. Sam was originally prescribed Percodan, an oxycodone-based analgesic, for his pain. Megan was given Vicodin, a hydrocodone-based painkiller. Both Sam and Megan would eventually end up on OxyContin, however, with starkly different results.

While athletes experience a greater percentage of injuries than do most other teenagers who remain off the field, unless their mishaps cause excruciating and chronic pain, they should not be prescribed OxyContin for fear they could develop an unnecessary dependency on the drug.

The drugs worked for a while. Soon though, as the pain persisted, Megan was limping, still unable to bend. She started taking more pills. Sam was also increasing the number of pills he was taking. Their bodies were building a tolerance to the drugs, which meant that they needed to take more and more pills to achieve the same relief. Eventually, Sam and Megan were both taking as many as ten pills each day.

DEVELOPING A DEPENDENCY

The difference between Sam and Megan is that his injury had healed and hers hadn't. Sam was no longer treating his back pain. He was feeding his dependence. He told his mother that he was still having pain, holding his back as if he was in discomfort. But other than his growing addiction, Sam was healthy. Meanwhile, in addition to her chronic hip pain, Megan had begun to experience numbness in her leg. This disabled her and forced her husband to stay home from work to care for her. Although only Megan needed powerful prescription drugs to ease her pain, both she and Sam were becoming addicts. The defining moment arrived when they sought new doctors.

Sam's first doctor was concerned with his overuse of Percodan, as well as the revealing fact that his current X-rays showed no damage to his back. Refusing to renew Sam's prescription, the doctor sent him away desperate for more pills. He had developed a mental and physical addiction to oxycodone. Sam soon visited another doctor in the next town, claiming he was experiencing pain. Sam's new doctor was more receptive, yet asked questions, took X-rays, and conducted tests. Sam moaned and groaned about how he needed painkillers, pointing to the area of his back where his injury had been. Although Sam's new doctor couldn't see the cause of his pain, he trusted Sam and gave him a prescription for OxyContin.

FROM DEPENDENCY TO ABUSE

Conversely, Megan admitted she was taking too many pills, so her husband took her to a pain specialist to find one single medication for her physical ailments. She was, in fact, a patient in chronic pain, suffering daily and in dire need. So, the specialist added OxyContin to her other medications. Soon, however, the doctor wanted her to take only one pill. He had to slowly ease her off the others. This seemed to be the cure: Megan felt great for the first time. Her limp was gone and she was up and about, doing housework, but still taking several pills each day. Her husband was amazed, and relieved, thinking that they'd finally treated her pain.

Meanwhile, Sam's new doctor was becoming concerned with his patient's continued use of OxyContin. He had good reason: Instead of just taking more pills than he needed, Sam was now using the drugs differently to get a greater, more instantaneous high. Sam was going through a one-month prescription of 100 OxyContin tablets in a few weeks. After the third prescription renewal, Sam's doctor warned him of the potential for addiction to oxycodone. The physician gave Sam one final prescription, but he didn't care. He could only think about getting more pills.

ADVERSE REACTIONS

There are a variety of complications that can result from abusing OxyContin. Among the most dangerous is respiratory depression,

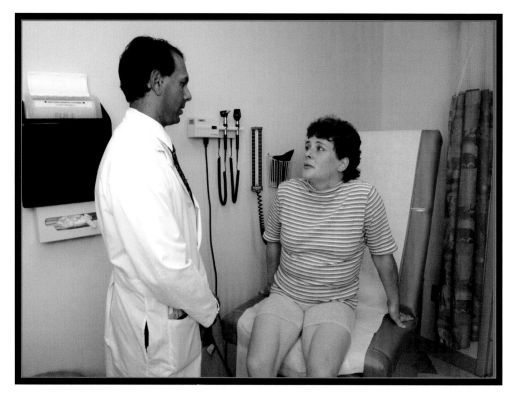

Doctor Jody Borgman *(left)* is vigilant about prescribing OxyContin to his patients. According to various studies conducted since 2000, many doctors find it difficult to assess their patients' pain levels, and some may not take a sufficient enough history to reveal a potential predisposition to addiction.

meaning that you can have difficulty breathing, or apnea, meaning you could stop breathing and go into respiratory arrest. If this happens, your heart could stop because you are not receiving any oxygen. Because it is nearly impossible to calculate how much of a dose could cause these effects, people should not experiment with prescription painkillers like OxyContin. Overdosing with OxyContin can also cause shock, circulatory depression, and hypotension, or low blood pressure.

Less serious complications from opiate abuse can include constipation, nausea, dizziness, vomiting, dry mouth, and headaches. In fact, due to all of these side effects, the U.S. Food and Drug Administration (FDA) has strengthened its warnings for Oxy-Contin. The Schedule II narcotic carries the strongest FDA labeling of any prescription drug on the market, its "black box warning."

FROM BAD TO WORSE

One day, Megan's husband came home from work to find his wife dead. The autopsy showed that she had died of an overdose from mixing her medications. Her body had simply given out. There had been no warning signs, only all of the "good" that the new drug, OxyContin, had done for his wife. Megan was buried the following weekend.

Sam didn't see the warning signs, either. He was too involved in his addiction for anything else. School suffered. He was failing several classes and on the verge of not graduating. Still, Sam was only concerned with getting his next dose. When his last prescription ran out, Sam tried to find another doctor but was turned away. Even his local pharmacy was getting suspicious of his need for so many prescriptions. Desperate, he cashed in a $10,000 savings bond for college to buy more OxyContin from illegal sources. It was easy. His friends knew where to get "O.C.," but it was far more expensive than from the pharmacy. Within weeks, the $10,000 was gone.

Sam's videogame and MP3 players were the next to go, followed by his mother's jewelry. Sam was getting good at lying, too, claiming that the house had been robbed. His mother was heartbroken. Her engagement ring and pearl necklace were gone, but at least Sam had pills. Soon, there was nothing else to steal.

Sam tried begging, but that only got him so far. Without access to cash, his friends refused him. They could get more than $1,000 for their parents' and grandparents' prescriptions without much effort, so Sam went to another dealer he'd only heard about. This guy was shady; Sam had never bought from him before. And when Sam said he only had a $20 bill, the dealer gave Sam a small baggy filled with a brown powder—heroin—instead of his usual white pill.

GETTING HELP

The heroin that Sam bought was bad. Just a few snorts made Sam's nose bleed. It wouldn't stop, but he still snorted more. Then, everything went black. Sam had overdosed.

Sam got lucky when his mother returned home early from work. She'd been worried about him, especially when police didn't believe his story of the robbery. When she found Sam unconscious, she knew that her son needed professional help. Sam's mother called 911 and got him admitted to the hospital, but he couldn't go home after he was released. Sam was forced to go into a rehabilitation center. Sam's mother took a second mortgage on her home to pay for his rehab. She'd lost everything, but she wasn't going to lose her son.

At rehab, Sam felt alone. But there were other kids and adults there, other users with similar stories. Judges who offered sentences in rehab centers rather than in jails had sent many people there for treatment. If the addicts didn't recover, the only alternative for them was prison. Once in rehab, former users were

Noelle Bush, daughter of Florida Governor Jeb Bush and niece of President George W. Bush, spent some time at this drug rehabilitation clinic in Orlando, Florida, in 2002. Many rehabilitation clinics across the United States are having difficulties meeting the demands of an increasing number of patients who have developed addictions to prescription drugs.

repeatedly tested, making sure they weren't using drugs. Most of them had stolen from their families, too. Sam wasn't alone at all, but he wanted to die.

The pain and discomfort from withdrawal was far worse than any injury. The back pain that had put Sam on prescription drugs was nothing compared to the pounding in his brain. He felt like he was being tortured. He was sweating and unable to move. One minute he felt like he was burning up, and the next minute, he was freezing. He vomited constantly as his body tried to rid itself of the drugs. For weeks, Sam hoped that he would die.

For all of the pain of withdrawal, Sam was lucky. His mother visited and told him she loved him. Most of the other addicts had no one; they'd stolen and lied so many times that their families had abandoned them. Even adults, who had once had careers, homes, and families, were now alone.

It took nearly a month for Sam's pain from withdrawal to stop. Strangely, though, the first few weeks out of rehab were even harder because Sam knew that he could easily get more pills. OxyContin was always available. Each time he thought about using, about how nice it would be to get numb, Sam would think of his mother and how hard she had struggled to help him. Then, he would think of all those people in rehab who had supported him, too. Although he wanted to get numb, he knew he couldn't take one more pill. One pill would lead to another, and maybe heroin, and then maybe prison. He'd been lucky—Sam knew that much.

CHAPTER 4
OxyContin and the Legal System

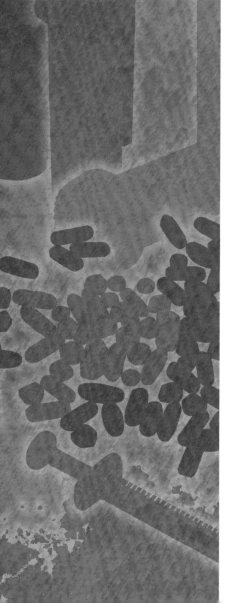

The battle over prescription drug abuse has many fronts: addicts, patients, doctors, pharmaceutical manufacturers and their lawyers, and law enforcement. The heated debate over OxyContin has even included Congress and the White House. It is clear that the OxyContin epidemic involves all Americans, with all sides laying blame, but none offering many solutions.

Law enforcement has approached prescription drug abuse differently than the abuse of other drugs. Historically, the DEA and local law enforcement agencies have targeted users and dealers, especially involving marijuana, cocaine, methamphetamine, and other illegal drugs. This has resulted in millions of individuals being arrested and sent to prison for years without any great reduction of the trade of illicit drugs.

With OxyContin, however, federal, state, and local officials have targeted doctors, the source of the prescriptions. Dozens of doctors have been investigated and arrested for writing prescriptions to known abusers. In the most severe instances, this has had a significant impact on the illegal sale and abuse of OxyContin. Still, the tendency of abusers to doctor shop has caught doctors in a legal web. Believing that they were treating patients with

Physician Ali Sawaf *(second from right)* is taken into custody in 2001 from his office in Harlan, Kentucky. Sawaf, the first physician to be arrested in a crackdown of federal and state law enforcement agencies, turned to illegally prescribing OxyContin and other painkillers to earn extra money after he lost his $250,000-a-year job at a regional clinic.

legitimate pain, many innocent doctors have been arrested for simply doing their jobs.

This problem has caused a major uproar in the medical community, especially since the DEA has admitted to targeting doctors who write prescriptions for opioids like OxyContin. Karen Tandy, the DEA administrator, officially stated that only 0.1 percent of the 600,000 doctors in the United States were investigated in 2005, equaling 600 doctors. However, Ronald Libby, a professor at the University of North Florida, puts instances of investigations much higher—at 17 percent annually. That's more than 100,000 doctors being investigated. The large gap between the DEA's and Libby's estimates are vast—more than 99,000. Perhaps the actual number falls somewhere in between, which reinforces the reality that the DEA is taking a hard

Physician Joan Jaszczult of Bloomfield, New Jersey, was among nine people arrested in a statewide OxyContin distribution ring in 2005. She was charged with writing the prescriptions for the ring for which she was paid in cash. Once in possession of the OxyContin pills, Jaszczult's "patients" sold them for huge profits.

look at doctors' habits. What none can question is the fact that dozens of medical professionals have been arrested and convicted, including at least five for manslaughter due to patients' deaths from overdose. Doctors aren't the only ones being blamed, however.

PURDUE PHARMA'S LIABILITY

In addition to doctors, the manufacturer of OxyContin, Purdue Pharma, is the focus of liable suits for the surge in OxyContin abuse in some cases. Mostly focused on the company's early marketing of OxyContin, which was cited as "overly aggressive" by the U.S. GAO in 2003, Purdue Pharma is now helping to educate the public about the potential for OxyContin abuse. One such liable case was settled in 2004. Perdue Pharma was ordered to pay $10 million to the West Virginia Attorney General's office to end a lawsuit that accused the company of illegally marketing OxyContin. This money is currently being used to help educate the public and to offset state costs for drug rehabilitation and prevention programs.

Lawyers representing OxyContin patients and addicts have filed hundreds of civil lawsuits against Purdue Pharma. And while many cases have been dismissed, the company still faces a few serious charges. Very few argue that Purdue Pharma overtouted the effectiveness of OxyContin with doctors while also downplaying the potential for addiction.

The cases that were dismissed were discounted because the company did not directly advertise OxyContin to the general public. Instead, Purdue Pharma marketed its product to doctors who are now being targeted by law enforcement.

In response to so much pressure, Purdue Pharma is introducing new versions of OxyContin with warnings on the packaging

The corporate office of Perdue Pharma, the drug maker who manufactures OxyContin in Stamford, Connecticut, is seen in this photograph. By 2001, Perdue Pharma was hit with thirteen different lawsuits from patients and patients' families who allege that the drug company should take responsibility for the alarming wave of overdoses and deaths among abusers of OxyContin.

about the drug's potential of addiction, as well as tablets that are more resilient to being altered. Most important, the company in 2004 released a "10-Point Program to Reduce Prescription Drug Abuse and Diversion Without Compromising Patient Access to Proper Pain Control." The program has been hailed by law enforcement officials as a proactive approach to confronting prescription drug abuse, but it does not fully address the current epidemic and its thousands of addicts.

REHAB INSTEAD OF INCARCERATION

Another change in law enforcement is being tested to address those who specifically become addicted to OxyContin. A new pharmaceutical task force has been created to target people who fraudulently feed their addictions through false prescriptions. The typical OxyContin addict isn't a violent criminal but will break the law to obtain the drug. Contrary to most people arrested for illegal drugs, OxyContin addicts caught by this task force are sent to a year-long program of drug testing, counseling, and rehabilitation. If an addict fails to complete the program, he or she is sent to jail. The message is clear: kick the addiction or face incarceration.

No matter the benefits of rehabilitation versus incarceration, law enforcement officials still do not yet specifically track Oxy-Contin or opioid deaths or arrests. Opioid statistics, OxyContin included, are combined for official tracking with all opiates, which greatly inflates the actual numbers. The result is alarming. There have been reports of more than 30,000 opiate-related fatalities since 2001. But this large number includes all heroin overdoses—a drug that often leads to overdose and death, as well as AIDS through shared hypodermic needles. Specific to OxyContin, fatalities from overdoses—mostly due to mixing other drugs and alcohol—are estimated at around 10,000 over the same period. Still startling high, the lack of accurate tracking undermines arguments for such strict enforcement.

For others, though, rehab programs came too late. OxyContin initially targeted rural regions, then suburbs and cities. Sadly, many abusers are now dead, or in jail. Armed robberies of pharmacies remain frequent, and legitimate patients often report having their OxyContin stolen by addicts. Rehabilitation may be too late for some addicts, but it is not too late to prevent future abuse, especially among teenagers.

AWARENESS AMONG PROFESSIONALS

Obviously, the greatest impact of the OxyContin epidemic is being felt within the medical community. Medical professionals and clinics are feeling the most strain. Rehabilitation clinics have been overwhelmed; a new clinic that opened in Arkansas in late 1993—before OxyContin even hit the market—reported that the majority of clients were there for opioid abuse. Another clinic in southwest Virginia reported that 80 percent of the 290 people in its outpatient treatment program named OxyContin as their primary drug of abuse. Heroin and OxyContin addiction and treatment go hand-in-hand; the same treatments used for heroin also work for OxyContin abusers. Long-term, residential, therapeutic treatments are available for all opioid addicts, as are medication-assisted outpatient programs.

However, one of the problems of the current epidemic is that OxyContin addicts are currently overwhelming methadone clinics, which were intended to serve only heroin addicts. Abusers of both drugs require professional help, and the recent spike in admissions has forced some states to sue Purdue Pharma to recover the extra cost of treating those people addicted to OxyContin such as the 2004 case mentioned earlier that was settled in West Virginia. Moreover, such widespread abuse has forced some hospitals and clinics to institute stronger control over OxyContin. An alliance of Cincinnati, Ohio, hospitals, for example, has restricted the use of OxyContin to cancer patients only, the intended market for the drug when it was developed.

As law enforcement officials and medical professionals take steps to limit the future spread of OxyContin abuse, the needs of those who truly require the relief of the drug must not be forgotten. There remains a legitimate use for OxyContin. As such, completely removing it from the market or placing overly harsh restrictions on its use will severely punish people with legitimate needs.

CHAPTER 5

Drug Abuse and Society: What Is the Impact?

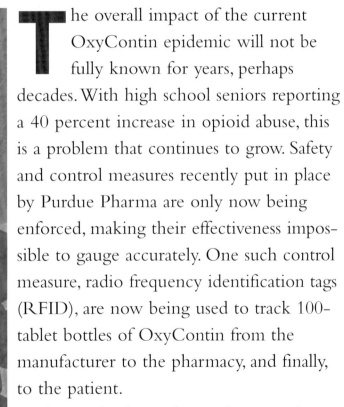

The overall impact of the current OxyContin epidemic will not be fully known for years, perhaps decades. With high school seniors reporting a 40 percent increase in opioid abuse, this is a problem that continues to grow. Safety and control measures recently put in place by Purdue Pharma are only now being enforced, making their effectiveness impossible to gauge accurately. One such control measure, radio frequency identification tags (RFID), are now being used to track 100-tablet bottles of OxyContin from the manufacturer to the pharmacy, and finally, to the patient.

Currently, due to law enforcement's aggressiveness in investigating doctors, many have stopped prescribing opioids. As a result, patients with real, chronic pain are going untreated because their doctors don't want to get investigated. Again, the outcome of this new approach to drug abuse enforcement won't be known for years, but it is clear that the DEA is taking any potential epidemic very seriously. Whether these efforts actually help remains questionable.

Charlie Crist *(left)*, Florida's attorney general, speaks with Teresa Ashcraft, a parent whose nineteen-year-old son, Bobby, died from overdosing on OxyContin, before the Symposium on Prescription Drug Abuse on February 4, 2004, in Tallahassee, Florida.

Still, methadone clinics are being overwhelmed with OxyContin addicts, costing large amounts of money and time, and straining the overall system. However welcome, "drug courts" are sending people caught using fake prescriptions for OxyContin to rehab instead of to jail, putting even more stress on recovery programs. Additional resources are required to meet the increased demand by current addicts, while even more will be necessary to care for future abusers.

Education and rehabilitation take time. And then there is the bigger question: Are cancer patients and chronic pain sufferers getting adequate treatment when doctors fear the potential legal ramifications of prescribing OxyContin?

A DIVISIVE DEBATE

The battle over the benefits of OxyContin versus potential abuse has incited a very public debate. Congress has held hearings. Doctors are concerned about the increased investigations by the DEA and are crying foul. Purdue Pharma is calling lawyers bringing lawsuits "ambulance chasers." And legitimate patients who need the drug are wondering how they can obtain it legally. As political as it is public, the debate over OxyContin continues. Addicts still need treatment, clinics are being overwhelmed, and those in pain are left suffering.

OxyContin has sparked a much larger debate about prescription drug use and abuse. Are corporate profits more important than public health? Are there too many drugs or too few accurate studies on their potential problems? Are teenagers abusing prescription drugs because they are so readily available? The answers may not become known for years. What is clear is that prescription drug use requires ongoing monitoring.

LONG-TERM UNKNOWNS

Perhaps the only benefit of the current OxyContin epidemic is a growing awareness about the rise in prescription drug abuse. Law enforcement agencies are more aware of the need for different approaches to recognizing and combating abuse. Doctors realize even more that they have to be careful to notice patterns of abuse in their patients. And pharmaceutical companies now see that they may be held liable for the drugs they produce. Finally, the public is learning more about the dangers of prescription drug abuse in general.

Because of these developments, tomorrow's potential epidemic may be avoided. Like OxyContin, if any powerful prescription drug is released without clear warnings to both doctors and patients, the resulting abuse may be blamed on the manufacturer. Doctors see too many patients—as well as pharmaceutical sales representatives—to fully screen every drug and person for weaknesses and potential problems. Meanwhile, people are still being inundated with television commercials for drugs: vague, cure-all messages that do nothing but try to convince them of the drugs' benefits.

Among the cures for prescription drug abuse is greater control over the companies that produce them, as well as more disclosure to the doctors who prescribe them. Too often, patients seeking legitimate medications overtly trust both the companies and their doctors. Pharmaceuticals aren't products; they are powerful drugs for specific ailments. Ultimately, people must take greater responsibility for what they put in their bodies, just as companies and medical professionals must be more judicious about who benefits from these "miracle" drugs.

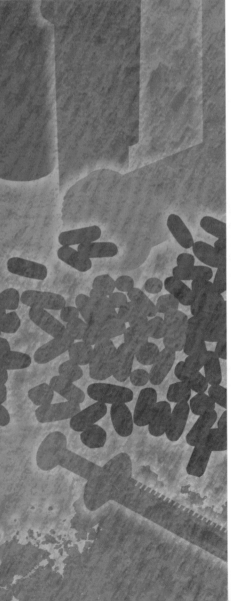

CHAPTER 6
OxyContin and the Media: Epidemic or Distortion?

As the debate over OxyContin and other prescription drugs continues, more articles are being published that frame each side of the battle. The *New York Times* calls the OxyContin epidemic a "distortion," claiming that too many doctors are being investigated and prosecuted without any firm data to support such enforcement.

Because opioids like OxyContin are combined with opiates in law enforcement data, a clear, hard case for fighting the problem is difficult to make and all too easy to undermine.

Since OxyContin abuse originated in rural regions, it didn't receive much notice at first. When it spread into suburbs and cities, however, abuse of the drug gained national attention. Today, the problem is often reported in the news. Various

Danny Osborne Jr., a coal miner from West Virginia, stands next to an anti-drug poster at a coal industry meeting in Hazard, Kentucky, on December 8, 2004. Osborne admitted to abusing OxyContin while a miner in central Appalachia.

government and medical studies attempt to uncover more about the drug and its users and abusers.

LEARNING FROM PAST EXPERIENCE

The impact of Purdue Pharma's marketing campaign for OxyContin cannot be ignored, but its efforts to educate the public will hopefully limit further increases in abuse. Also, the lack of opioid-specific data could force law enforcement to be more vigilant in tracking all drug-related deaths, arrests, and convictions.

The public has the most to learn, however. There is no such thing as a "miracle" pill. Aggressively marketing medicine can confuse anyone, which should make patients, parents, and teenagers much more eager to seek information. Most important, prescription drugs should get as much media attention for the dangers they present than any cures they promise. Medicine should only be taken as directed by those for whom it's prescribed. Finally, medicine cabinets in homes with young children and teens should be locked.

Instead of debating whether OxyContin is an epidemic or not, medical professionals and policy makers should discuss how to prevent the next wave of prescription drug abuse. Parents, doctors, pharmaceutical companies, and the media must all be involved in this nationwide discussion. The damage to our society from OxyContin abuse continues. Let us not repeat past mistakes. We have too much to lose.

GLOSSARY

addiction The state of habitually or compulsively consuming or ingesting a substance such as drugs, food, and/or cigarettes.

chronic Long-lasting and recurring.

liable Being held responsible.

methadone A synthetic (human-made) opiate used to treat heroin and OxyContin addictions.

opiate A drug such as codeine or morphine whose origin is the natural opium poppy.

opioid A drug such as OxyContin whose origin is a synthetic opiate.

oxycodone A semi-synthetic painkiller like morphine that is the base of drugs such as Percodan, Percocet, and Tylox.

susceptibility A state of being easily affected.

tolerance A condition where a person requires more and more of a drug or substance to get the same result.

withdrawal The mental and physical experience of detoxification that a person goes through when he or she is no longer taking a drug after being addicted to it.

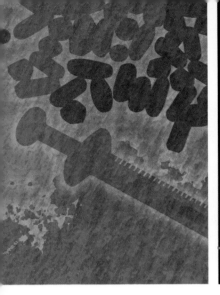

American Council for Drug
  Education
164 West 74th Street
New York, NY 10023
(800) 488-3784
Web site: http://www.acde.org

Canadian Centre on Substance
  Abuse (CCSA)
75 Albert Street, Suite 300
Ottawa, ON K1P 5E7
Canada
(613) 235-4048
Web site: http://www.ccsa.ca

Center for Substance Abuse
  Treatment Information and
  Treatment Referral Hotline

11426-28 Rockville Pike
Suite 410
Rockville, MD 20852
(800) 662-HELP
(800) 66-AYUDA (Spanish)

Community Anti-Drug
  Coalitions of America
  (CADCA)
625 Slaters Lane, Suite 300
Alexandria, VA 22314
(800) 54-CADCA (542-2322)
Web site: http://
  www.cadca.org

Narcotics Anonymous (NA)
World Service Office
P.O. Box 9999

Van Nuys, CA 91409
(818) 773-9999
Web site: http://www.na.org

National Clearinghouse for
   Alcohol and Drug
   Information (NCADI)
P.O. Box 2345
Rockville, MD 20847-2345
(800) 729-6686
(800) 767-8432 (Spanish)
Web site: http://
   ncadi.samhsa.gov

National Council on
   Alcoholism and Drug
   Dependence, Inc. (NCADD)
22 Cortlandt Street, Suite 801
New York, NY 10007-3128
(212) 269-7797
Web site: http://www.ncadd.org

Teen Challenge USA
P.O. Box 1015
Springfield, MO 65801
(417) 862-6969
Web site: http://
   teenchallengeusa.com/
   index.asp

WEB SITES

Due to the changing nature
of Internet links, Rosen
Publishing has developed an
online list of Web sites related
to the subject of this book.
This site is updated regularly.
Please use this link to access
the list:

http://www.rosenlinks.com/
   das/oxyc

FOR FURTHER READING

Bayer, Linda N., and Austin Sarat. *Drugs, Crime, and Criminal Justice* (Crime, Justice, and Punishment). New York, NY: Chelsea House, 2001.

Fitzhugh, Karla. *Prescription Drug Abuse* (What's the Deal?). Chicago, IL: Heinmann, 2005.

Fooks, Louie. *The Drug Trade: The Impact on Our Lives* (21st Century Debates). Chicago, IL: Raintree, 2003.

Foster, Olive M. *Prescription Pain Relievers* (Drugs: The Straight Facts). Philadelphia, PA: Chelsea House, 2005.

Lookadoo, Justin. *The Dirt on Drugs* (A Dateable Book). Grand Rapids, MI: Revell, 2005.

Pinsky, Drew. *When Painkillers Become Dangerous: What Everyone Needs to Know About OxyContin and Other Prescription Drugs.* Center City, MN: Hazelden, 2004.

Roberts, Jeremy. *Prescription Drug Abuse* (Drug Abuse Prevention Library). New York, NY: Rosen Publishing, 2000.

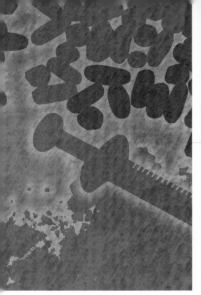

BIBLIOGRAPHY

American Psychiatric Association. *Diagnostic and Statistical Manual of Mental Disorders*, 4th ed. Washington, DC: Author, 1994.

Arnold, Chris. "Teen Abuse of Painkiller OxyContin on the Rise." National Public Radio. Retrieved March 2006 (http://www.npr.org/templates/story/story.php?storyId=5061674).

Cantlupe, Joe, and David Hasemyer. "Accidental Addicts." *San Diego Union-Tribune*. Retrieved March 2006 (http://www.signonsandiego.com/uniontrib/20040926/news_mz1n26pills.html).

Crimaldi, Laura. "Prescription for Addiction: OxyContin Boom: Side Effects." *Boston Herald*. Retrieved March 2006. (http://news.bostonherald.com/localregional/view.bg?articleid=121395).

Gilson, A. M., K. M. Ryan, D. E. Joranson, and J. L. Dahl. "A Reassessment of Trends in the Medical Use and Abuse of Opioid Analgesics and Implications for Diversion Control: 1997–2002." *Journal of Pain and Symptom Management*, Vol. 28, 2004, pp. 176-188.

Hammack, Laurence. "FDA to Hold OxyContin Hearings." *Roanoke Times*. Retrieved March 2006 (http://www.roanoke.com/roatimes/news/story117714.html).

Katz, D. A., and L. R. Hays. "Adolescent OxyContin Abuse." *Journal of the American Academy of Child and Adolescent Psychiatry*, Vol. 43, 2004, pp. 231-234.

Miller, N. S., and A. Greenfeld. "Patient Characteristics and Risk Factors for Development of Dependence on Hydrocodone and Oxycodone." *American Journal of Therapeutics*, Vol. 11, 2004, pp. 26–32.

Office of Applied Studies. Results from the 2003 National Survey on Drug Use and Health: National Findings. Rockville, MD: Substance Abuse and Mental Health Services Administration, 2004.

Potter, J. S., G. Hennessey, J. A. Borrow, S. F. Greenfield, and R. D. Weiss. "Substance Use Histories in Patients Seeking Treatment for Controlled-Release Oxycodone Dependence." *Drug and Alcohol Dependence*, Vol. 76, 2004, pp. 213–215.

Purdue Pharma L.P. "Purdue Pharma's 10-Point Program to Reduce Prescription Drug Abuse and Diversion Without Compromising Patient Access to Proper Pain Control." September 2005. Retrieved March 2006 (http://www.purduepharma.com/pressroom/app/news_announc/ss_10ptPlan.asp).

U.S. Department of Health and Human Services. *OxyContin: Prescription Drug Abuse*. April 2001.

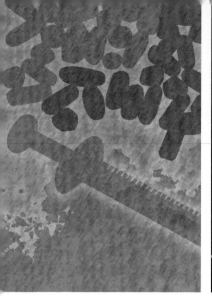

INDEX

ABOUT THE AUTHOR

Brad Lockwood is an award-winning author of fiction and nonfiction books. His writings on politics and public affairs also regularly appear in national magazines and newspapers. As a father of a soon-to-be teenager, he appreciates the opportunity to write about various topics for young readers, educating students about drug abuse and addiction, government policy, and other timely subjects. Lockwood lives in Brooklyn, NY.

PHOTO CREDITS

P. 5 © David McNew/Getty Images; p. 8 © Darren McCollester/Getty Images; p. 12 © Gaetano/Corbis; p. 15 NCI Clinical Center/Matthews Media Group; pp. 18, 42, 45, 50, 55 © AP/Wide World Photos; p. 23 © Jose Luis Pelaez, Inc./Corbis; p. 25 © William Thomas Cain/Getty Images; p. 33 © Paul A. Souders/Corbis; p. 36 KRT/Newscom; p. 39 © Chris Livingston/Getty Images; p. 43 © Tony Kurdzuk/Star Ledger/Corbis.

Designer: Tahara Anderson; Editor: Joann Jovinelly
Photo Researcher: Nicole DiMella